Fresh & Tast...

Fast
fresh food

R&R PUBLICATIONS MARKETING PTY LTD

Published by:
R&R Publications Marketing Pty Ltd
ABN 78 348 105 138
PO Box 254, Carlton North, Victoria 3054, Australia
Phone (61 3) 9381 2199 Fax (61 3) 9381 2689
E-mail: info@randrpublications.com.au
Website: www.randrpublications.com.au
Australia-wide toll-free: 1800 063 296

Fresh & Tasty Fast fresh food

Publisher: Richard Carroll
Creative Director: Aisling Gallagher
Cover Designer: Lucy Adams
Typeset by Elain Wei Voon Loh
Production Manager: Anthony Carroll
Food Photography: Steve Baxter, Phillip Wilkins, David Munns, Thomas Odulate,
Christine Hanscomb and Frank Wieder
Home Economists: Sara Buenfeld, Emma Patmore, Nancy McDougall, Louise Pickford,
Jane Stevenson, Oded Schwartz, Alison Austin and Jane Lawrie
Food Stylists: Helen Payne, Sue Russell, Sam Scott, Antonia Gaunt and Oded Schwartz
Recipe Development: Terry Farris, Jacqueline Bellefontaine,
Becky Johnson, Valerie Barrett, Emma Patmore, Geri Richards,
Pam Mallender and Jan Fullwood
Proofreader: Kate Evans

Disclaimer: The nutritional information listed with each recipe does not include the nutrient content
of garnishes or any accompaniments not listed in specific quantities in the ingredient list. The
nutritional information for each recipe is an estimate only, and may vary depending on the brand of
ingredients used, and due to natural biological variations in the composition of natural foods such as
meat, fish, fruit and vegetables. The nutritional information was calculated by using the computer
program Foodworks dietary analysis software (version 3.01, Xyris Software Pty Ltd Queensland
Australia), and is based on the Australian food composition tables and food manufacturers' data.
Where not specified, ingredients are always analysed as average or medium, not small or large.
The analysis shown is for 100g of the recipe specified.

Includes Index
ISBN 1 74022 439 6
EAN 9 781740 224 390

First edition printed January 2006
This edition printed September 2009
Computer Typeset in Futura

Printed in Singapore

Cover: Feta and Ricotta Stuffed Tomatoes, page 59

26

Contents

60

66

Introduction

The rise of fast food has seen many people scrambling to the phone in between appointments or at the end of a long work day to find a quick fix for their hunger pangs. However, there has been a rapid return to homemade cooking as people realise that there's something about food made in your own kitchen that can't be duplicated in a commercial establishment: it gives you a good feeling to know you've prepared a tasty meal for yourself and your family.

Our challenge has been to compile a collection of recipes that are quick and easy to prepare, but take no shortcuts on taste. We believe we've achieved this tall order with outstanding variety. All our recipes have been tried and tested by our talented team of experts so you can be sure they'll turn out exactly the way they appear in the pictures – simply sensational. Take a few moments to meander through this book. Our recipes will tantalise your senses and make you eager to indulge in the next experience.

Take a straightforward sausage sizzle, T-Bone steak or lamb satay kebab, for example. It takes only minutes to cook these meals yourself; serve them fresh to your family on your own table or outside in the hot weather during a barbecue with friends. Find out how to prepare them properly and you'll avoid overcooking or drowning them in an imbalance of seasonings that detract from the pleasure that can be given by these favourite, simple foods. Small variations can make a world of difference; the average will become the spectacular after we have shown you how to strike the right balance.

Perhaps you want to make something with an air of style and sophistication, without slaving over a hot oven for hours. Our seafood selection will surprise you with unique combinations of flavours – such as shellfish and rocket pizzas and salmon with pineapple salsa – all of which can be put together in the same time it takes to fry up a burger and chips. But rather than feel disappointed that you have just fed your body a fatty meal, with these recipes you can feast on a fabulous fare without regrets.

We've taken all the goodness of nature and brought it into your kitchen in each recipe. A wonderful asparagus and lemon risotto or beef fillet with wild mushrooms will leave a pleasant sensation in your stomach. Best of all, they're uncomplicated and help you avoid the trap of the 'fast-food lifestyle'.

New Confidence

Our delectable dishes leave you with the feeling that you can turn your skills into the expertise of a seasoned chef. The advice given by our experts in each set of instructions is carefully considered so you get the result you seek with minimum effort. You'll approach each page of this cookbook with enthusiasm as you embark on a journey of creative cuisine. You'll start to gain knowledge of how ingredients work together to take on a whole new appearance and a bold new taste.

Best of all, you'll gain a new confidence when hosting guests because you know you can treat them to a wonderful meal and still spend most of your time enjoying their company. No more running around behind the scenes to present a seemingly effortless three-course meal. No more wondering whether what you see in cookbook images is really the reward for your effort. We take the stress out of hosting and ensure you make it a frequent occasion. Cooking is not complicated when you have our recipes at your fingertips.

From starters to desserts, we have every course covered. Try various combinations on your family and friends and you'll start to hear more and more compliments. Sticking to old

favourites can be comforting, but why not splash out and try something out of the ordinary? For instance, start with chicken and corn chowder, move onto Lebanese lamb rolls and top it off with mini chocolate muffins with mocha Sauce. Or perhaps you might like some other combination, such as beetroot, pear and bitter-leaf salad, fettuccine carbonara and raspberry and eelderflower fool. The possibilities are limited only by your willingness to move away from the mundane towards something more appealing.

It's our absolute pleasure to take the burden out of homemade meals and make delicious delights accessible to even the person most pressed for time. This book will spare you from all the guilt of money spent on expensive restaurant meals and fat-filled fast food and bring many friends to your door in search of good food and great company.

Enjoy!

Soups, Salads and Starters

There's no need to forsake the pleasure of homemade cooking for a busy lifestyle if you know how to make a scrumptious soup, salad or starter in just minutes. Our compilation of recipes will ensure you avoid the traps of take-away meals that are loaded with calories. From the goodness of a greek salad to the simple pleasure of coconut, sweet potato and spinach soup, this section will firm your resolve to enjoy nothing less than the best of quick-and-easy cuisine.

Coconut, Sweet Potato, and Spinach Soup

Preparation 10 mins **Cooking** 25 mins **Calories** 289 **Fat** 4g

2 tbsps butter
455g sweet potatoes, cut into 1cm dice
1 onion, chopped
2 cloves garlic, crushed
1 tsp grated root ginger
1 tbsp medium curry paste
2½ cups vegetable stock
1 cup coconut milk
juice of 1 lime
½ tsp dried crushed chillies
3 cups fresh spinach, shredded
salt and black pepper

1 Melt the butter in a saucepan and fry the sweet potatoes, onion, garlic, ginger and curry paste for 5 minutes or until lightly golden.

2 Add the stock, coconut milk, lime juice and chilli. Bring to the boil, cover and simmer for 15 minutes or until the sweet potatoes are tender.

3 Leave the soup to cool a little, then purée half of it with a hand blender. Return the purée to the pan, add the spinach and cook for 1–2 minutes, until the spinach has just wilted and the soup has heated through. Season to taste.

Serves 4

Note: Sweet potatoes have a slightly nutty flavour. They also make the texture of this soup really creamy. For a fantastic light meal, serve the soup with naan bread.

Lemon and Herb Basted Scallops

Preparation 10 mins **Cooking** 5 mins **Calories** 125 **Fat** 10g

4 tbsps butter, melted
2 tbsps lemon juice
1 clove garlic, crushed
1 tsp basil, finely chopped
1 tsp coriander, finely chopped
1 tsp mint, finely chopped
500g package frozen scallops
1 red onion, cut into wedges
1 red capsicum, cut into triangles
watercress
lemon wedges

1 Combine the butter, lemon juice, garlic and herbs and set aside.

2 Thread scallops, onion and capsicum onto skewers and brush with the butter mixture.

3 Place the skewers onto a preheated grill plate turning once and brushing with butter mixture, until scallops are just cooked (approximately 5 minutes).

4 Serve garnished with watercress and lemon wedges.

Serves 6

Cheese and Herb Salad

Preparation 10 mins **Cooking** nil **Calories** 120 **Fat** 19g

500g baked ricotta cheese, chopped

2 tomatoes, cut into wedges

90g marinated olives

440g canned artichoke hearts, drained and quartered

375g assorted lettuce leaves

4 tbsps mixed fresh herb leaves, such as coriander, parsley, sage and chives

3 tbsps balsamic or red-wine vinegar

185g croûtons

1 Arrange ricotta cheese, tomatoes, olives, artichoke hearts, lettuce leaves and herbs on a serving platter. Sprinkle with vinegar, scatter with croûtons and serve immediately.

Serves 4

Serving suggestion: Italian breadsticks make an interesting accompaniment to this Italian-inspired salad.

Note: Baked ricotta cheese is available from Italian food stores and good cheese shops. If it is unavailable feta cheese is a good alternative.

Greek Salad

Preparation 10 mins **Cooking** nil **Calories** 360 **Fat** 9g

1 lettuce, leaves separated
and shredded
2 tomatoes, sliced
1 small cucumber, sliced
1 red capsicum, cut into thin strips
1 small onion, thinly sliced
1 cup feta cheese, cut into small cubes
12 black olives

Lemon and Mint Dressing
6 tbsps olive oil
2 tbsps lemon juice
2 tsps chopped fresh mint
2 tsps chopped fresh marjoram
salt and black pepper

1 Line a large serving platter or salad bowl with the lettuce. Top with the tomatoes, cucumber, capsicum, onion, feta and olives.

2 To make the dressing, place oil, lemon juice, mint and marjoram in a screwtop jar and season to taste. Shake well. Spoon over the salad. Serve immediately.

Serves 4

Carrot and Sweet Potato Soup

Preparation 10 mins **Cooking** 40 mins **Calories** 276 **Fat** 4g

2 tbsp butter
1 large onion, chopped
3 large carrots, chopped
1 large sweet potato, chopped
4 cups chicken or vegetable stock
³/₄ cup sour cream
2 tbsps chopped fresh dill

1 Melt the butter in a saucepan over a medium heat. Add the onion, carrots and sweet potato. Cook for 5 minutes.

2 Stir in the stock. Bring to the boil. Simmer for 30 minutes. Cool slightly.

3 Purée the soup. Return the soup to a clean saucepan. Stir in the sour cream. Cook, without boiling, stirring constantly, for 5 minutes or until the soup is hot. Stir in the dill. Serve immediately.

Serves 4

Chicken and Corn Chowder

Preparation 10 mins **Cooking** 30 mins **Calories** 320 **Fat** 6g

1 tbsp vegetable oil

1 small onion, diced

255g boneless chicken breast fillets, shredded

3 potatoes, chopped

3 cups chicken stock

1½ cups canned corn kernels, drained and chopped

1¼ cups milk

1 bay leaf

freshly ground black pepper

1 tbsp lemon juice

2 tbsps chopped, fresh parsley

1 tbsp snipped fresh chives

½ cup grated Parmesan cheese

1 Heat the oil in a saucepan over a medium heat, add the onion and cook, stirring, for 4–5 minutes or until the onion is soft. Add the chicken and cook for 2 minutes longer or until the chicken just changes colour.

2 Add the potatoes and stock and bring to the boil. Reduce the heat and simmer for 10 minutes or until the potatoes are almost cooked. Stir the corn, milk, bay leaf and pepper to taste into the stock mixture and bring to a boil. Reduce the heat and simmer for 3–4 minutes or until the potatoes are cooked. Remove the bay leaf. Stir in the lemon juice, parsley, chives and pepper to taste. Just prior to serving, sprinkle with the Parmesan.

Serves 6

Note: To chop the corn, place in a food processor or blender and process using the pulse button until the corn is coarsely chopped. Creamed sweetcorn can be used in place of the kernels if you wish. If using creamed corn there's no need to chop it.

Gnocchi with Mascarpone and Blue Cheese

Preparation 5 mins **Cooking** 10 mins **Calories** 460 **Fat** 8g

400g fresh gnocchi
1 tbsp pine nut kernels
1/2 cup mascarpone cheese
1 cup gorgonzola cheese, crumbled
salt and black pepper

1 Cook the gnocchi according to the packet instructions. Drain well, then transfer to a shallow flameproof dish.

2 Preheat the grill to high. Place the pine nut kernels in the grill pan and toast for 2–3 minutes, stirring from time to time, until golden. Keep an eye on them, as they can burn quickly.

3 Meanwhile, put the mascarpone and gorgonzola in a saucepan and warm over a very low heat, stirring, until melted. Season to taste. Spoon over the gnocchi, then grill for 2–3 minutes, until bubbling and golden. Scatter with the pine nut kernels and serve.

Serves 4

Note: Creamy mascarpone and gorgonzola produce this meltingly good Italian gnocchi dish. It's ideal served with a lightly dressed green or mixed salad.

Beetroot, Pear and Bitter-Leaf Salad

Preparation 15 mins **Cooking** 5 mins **Calories** 354 **Fat** 8g

½ cup walnut pieces

255g mixed salad leaves, including radicchio and frisée

225g beetroot, cooked in natural juices and sliced

2 pears, quartered, cored and sliced

45g Parmesan cheese

fresh chives to garnish

Dressing

2 tbsps chopped fresh herbs, including basil, chives, mint and parsley

4 tbsp walnut oil

2 tbsps extra virgin olive oil

1 clove garlic, crushed

2 tsps red-wine vinegar

1 tsp clear honey

salt and black pepper

1 Preheat the grill to high. To make the dressing, blend the herbs, oils, garlic, vinegar and honey until smooth in a food processor or with a hand blender. Season to taste.

2 Place the walnuts on a baking sheet and grill for 2–3 minutes, until golden, turning often. Arrange the leaves, beet and pear slices on serving plates. Scatter with the walnuts, then shave over thin slivers of Parmesan, using a vegetable peeler. Spoon the dressing over the salad, garnish with the whole chives and serve.

Serves 4

Note: Slightly bitter radicchio and frisée leaves are set off by sweet beet and pears. If preparing the salad ahead of time, toss the pears in lemon juice to stop them browning.

Tomato and Mozzarella Salad

Preparation 10 mins **Cooking** 5 mins **Calories** 306 **Fat** 7g

6 plum tomatoes, sliced

1 cup mozzarella cheese, drained and sliced

2 green onions, sliced

6 tbsps black olives

salt and black pepper

Dressing

3 tbsps extra virgin olive oil

1 clove garlic, crushed

2 tsps balsamic vinegar

2 tbsps chopped fresh basil

1. Arrange the tomatoes, mozzarella, green onions and olives in layers on serving plates and season to taste.

2. To make the dressing, heat the oil and garlic in a small saucepan over a very low heat for 2 minutes or until the garlic has softened but not browned. Remove the pan from the heat, add the vinegar and basil, then pour over the salad and serve.

Serves 4

Note: This classic Italian salad never fails to please and the hot dressing works really well with it. Don't skimp on the fresh basil or balsamic vinegar – it won't be the same.

Clam and Black Mussel Broth

Preparation 10 mins **Cooking** 40 mins **Calories** 133 **Fat** trace

3 tbsps vegetable oil

1 onion, finely chopped

2 tbsps Tom Yum paste

225g surf clams, cleaned and sandless

225g black mussels, cleaned

1 cup chicken stock

1 stalk lemon grass, chopped

juice of 1 lime

1 tbsp coriander stalk and roots, finely chopped

1 tbsp Thai fish sauce

1 tbsp coriander leaves, roughly chopped

1 Heat the oil in a wok or large cooking pot. Add the onion, Tom Yum, clams and mussels. Simmer, covered with a lid for 30 seconds.

2 Add chicken stock, lemon grass, lime juice, coriander stalk and roots and Thai fish sauce and stir through. Cook until all the shells have opened and discard any mussel shells that don't open.

3 Add the fresh coriander leaves and serve in soup bowls.

Serves 6

Caesar Salad with Crispy Prosciutto

Preparation 15 mins **Cooking** 15 mins **Calories** 313 **Fat** 5g

11cm slices day-old bread, cut into
1cm cubes

4 large slices prosciutto

2 lettuce cos, torn into
bite-sized pieces

1/2 cup Parmesan cheese, grated, plus
extra to serve (optional)

Dressing

8 anchovies, drained and mashed

2 tbsp extra virgin olive oil

3 tbsps reduced-calorie mayonnaise

1 clove garlic, crushed

1 tsp white-wine vinegar

1/2 tsp Worcestershire sauce

freshly ground black pepper

1   Preheat the oven. To make the croûtons, place the bread cubes on a baking tray and cook for 10–12 minutes, turning occasionally, until crisp and golden.

2   Preheat the grill to high. Grill the prosciutto for 1 minute or until very crisp, then leave to cool for 2 minutes. Place the lettuce leaves, croûtons and Parmesan in a bowl.

3   To make the dressing, put the anchovies, oil, mayonnaise, garlic, vinegar, Worcestershire sauce and pepper into a bowl and whisk until smooth. Spoon over the lettuce and croûtons, then toss until well coated. Top with the crispy prosciutto and extra Parmesan (if using) and serve.

Serves 4

Note: Even the classic Caesar salad can be improved upon. Here, grilled prosciutto adds extra crunch and a dash of Worcestershire sauce peps up the traditional dressing.

Oven temperature 200°C, 400°F, Gas 6

Vine Tomatoes and Goat's Cheese Bruschetta

Preparation 10 mins **Cooking** 20 mins **Calories** 278 **Fat** 6g

455g small vine-ripened tomatoes

2 tbsps extra virgin olive oil

1 clove garlic, crushed

4 sprigs fresh thyme

4 thick slices ciabatta bread, cut diagonally

4 tbsps ready-made tapenade

$\frac{1}{2}$ cup soft goat's cheese, cut into chunks

fresh basil leaves to garnish

1 Preheat the oven. Place the tomatoes, still on the vine, in a roasting tin and drizzle over the oil. Scatter over the garlic and thyme sprigs. Roast for 15 minutes or until the tomatoes are tender. Divide the tomatoes into 4 portions roughly equal, each still attached to part of the vine.

2 Meanwhile, preheat the grill to high. Toast the bread on both sides until golden. Spread each slice with 1 tablespoon of tapenade, add a few chunks of goat's cheese and top with the tomatoes on the vine. Drizzle over the juices from the roasting tin, sprinkle with the basil leaves and serve.

Serves 4

Note: The tapenade in this dish is full of strong Mediterranean flavours – capers, anchovies and olives. You can use loose cherry tomatoes, but cook them for a few minutes less.

Oven temperature 220°C, 440°F, Gas 7

Meat and Poultry

Take a trip to your local butcher with our serving suggestions in mind and you'll be delighted at how easily you can put together a delectable dish with minimum effort and maximum results. From Cajun chops to teriyaki tenderloins, meat and poultry tossed with seasoning is thoroughly enjoyable and so simple to prepare. Whether to add an exciting element to a barbecue or to surprise your family with a tasty new dish, take a browse through the following pages for inspiration. You'll be convinced that you can balance your work commitments with your love of homemade cooking and enjoy the best of both worlds.

Lamb with Mint Butter and Saffron Mash

Preparation 10 mins + 5 mins standing **Cooking** 25 mins **Calories** 808 **Fat** 7g

910g floury potatoes cut into chunks
salt and black pepper
2 tbsps butter, softened
2 tbsps chopped fresh mint, plus extra leaves to garnish
½ tsp ground cumin
4 tbsps light cream
pinch of saffron strands
4 lamb leg steaks

1 Cook the potatoes in a large saucepan of lightly salted water for 15 minutes or until tender. Meanwhile, mash together half the butter with the mint, cumin and a little pepper, then cover and refrigerate. Put the cream and saffron in a small pan, gently heat through, then remove from the heat and let stand for 5 minutes to infuse.

2 Preheat the grill to high. Season the lamb steaks and grill for 4–5 minutes each side, or until done to your liking. Cover with foil and leave to rest for 5 minutes. Meanwhile, drain the potatoes well and mash with a potato masher, then mix in the remaining butter and the saffron cream and season.

3 Divide the chilled mint butter between the steaks and grill for a few seconds until it melts. Serve the steaks with the saffron mash and pan juices. Garnish with the mint.

Serves 4

Note: Creamy saffron mash and mint butter turn juicy lamb steaks into a wonderful meal. Serve this dish with some fresh green vegetables.

Spiced Pork with Hummus and Coriander Oil

Preparation 10 mins + 5 mins standing **Cooking** 15 mins **Calories** 548 **Fat** 9g

4 pork fillets, about 225g each
1 tbsp olive oil
1 tsp paprika
½ tsp cayenne pepper
290g of fresh hummus
lemon wedges to serve
coriander leaves to garnish

Coriander Oil
4 tbsps extra virgin olive oil
2 green onions, finely chopped
1 tbsp chopped coriander leaves
salt and black pepper

1. Preheat the oven. Wipe the pork with damp kitchen towels. Mix the oil with the paprika and cayenne pepper. Rub over the pork fillets.

2. Heat a heavy-based frying pan, add the pork and fry for 2 minutes, turning, until seared all over. Add 2 tablespoons of water, cover and simmer for 10 minutes. Remove from the heat and let stand for 5 minutes. Put the hummus into a baking dish and place in the oven for 10 minutes to heat through.

3. Meanwhile, make the coriander oil. Heat the oil in a small pan, add the green onions and coriander and cook for 3–4 minutes, until the green onions have softened. Cool slightly, season, then blend until fairly smooth in a food processor or with a hand blender. Serve the pork in slices with the hummus, coriander oil and lemon wedges. Garnish with the coriander.

Serves 4

Note: The sunny flavours of the Mediterranean have inspired this pork dish. It's good served with pita bread.

Oven temperature 180°C, 350°F, Gas 4

Honeyed Gammon with Pineapple Salsa

Preparation 15 mins **Cooking** 10 mins **Calories** 535 **Fat** 6g

4 thick smoked ham steaks, about
225g each
2 sprigs fresh thyme
1 tbsp clear honey
lime wedges to serve
coriander leaves to garnish

Salsa
2 tomatoes
225g pineapple, cut into 1cm cubes
1 clove garlic, crushed
1 red chilli, deseeded and chopped
2 tbsps extra virgin olive oil
juice of ½ lime
2 tbsps chopped coriander leaves
salt and black pepper

1 First make the salsa. Put the tomatoes in a bowl and cover with boiling water. Leave for 30 seconds, then skin, deseed and dice. Combine with the pineapple, garlic, chilli, oil, lime juice and coriander. Season to taste and set aside.

2 Preheat the grill to high. Score the fat around the edge of each steak and rub all over with the thyme sprigs. Brush with honey and grill the ham for 2–3 minutes each side, until tender and cooked through. Serve with the salsa and lime wedges and garnish with the coriander.

Serves 4

Note: This is not the usual version of ham and pineapple! A spicy pineapple salsa really sets the steaks alight. Serve with either rice or potatoes and a fresh green salad.

Beef Fillet with Wild Mushrooms

Preparation 10 mins + 15 mins soaking **Cooking** 20 mins **Calories** 436 **Fat** 6g

15g dried porcini mushrooms
6 tbsps butter
4 beef fillet steaks
3 cups mixed fresh wild mushrooms, sliced
1 clove garlic, crushed
1 tsp chopped fresh thyme, plus extra to garnish
½ cup red wine
½ cup beef stock
salt and black pepper

1 Preheat the oven. Cover the dried mushrooms with 85mL of boiling water. Soak for 15 minutes or until softened. Strain, reserving the soaking liquid, then chop the mushrooms. Melt half a tablespoon of the butter and fry the steaks for 2–3 minutes each side, until browned. Wrap loosely in foil and keep warm in the oven.

2 Add half a tablespoon of the butter to the pan and fry the fresh mushrooms, dried mushrooms, garlic and thyme for 4 minutes or until the fresh mushrooms have softened. Add the wine, increase the heat and boil for 1–2 minutes, until the sauce has reduced by half.

3 Mix the dried mushroom soaking liquid with the beef stock, then add to the pan and simmer for 3 minutes. Stir in the remaining butter and season. Serve with the steaks, garnished with the thyme.

Serves 4

Note: Fillet steak, red wine and mushrooms is a much-loved combination. Here, both dried and fresh mushrooms are used to give the sauce an intense flavour.

Oven temperature 160°C, 325°F, Gas 3

Chicken Parcels with Tarragon Cream Sauce

Preparation 10 mins **Cooking** 35 mins **Calories** 545 **Fat** 8g

4 large skinless boneless
chicken breasts
8 sun-dried tomatoes in oil, drained
8 strips rindless smoked bacon
2 tbsps olive oil
455g baby leeks
1$\frac{1}{2}$ cups fresh chicken stock
2 tbsps brandy
$\frac{2}{3}$ cup light cream
2 tbsps chopped fresh tarragon,
plus extra to garnish
salt and black pepper

1 Preheat the oven. Cut a deep slice into 1 side of each chicken breast to make a pocket. Place 2 tomatoes in each pocket, then wrap 2 bacon strips around each breast. Secure with wetted cocktail sticks.

2 Heat 1 tablespoon of the oil in an ovenproof frying pan. Cook the chicken for 2–3 minutes, turning once, until browned all over. Transfer to the oven and cook for 15 minutes or until the chicken is cooked through. Transfer to a plate, remove the cocktail sticks and keep warm. Meanwhile, preheat the grill to high. Brush the leeks with the remaining oil and grill for 6–8 minutes, until softened.

3 Meanwhile, add the stock and brandy to the frying pan. Cook over a high heat for 3 minutes, stirring and scraping, until reduced by half. Whisk in the cream and tarragon and simmer for 2–3 minutes, until slightly thickened. Season, then spoon over the chicken parcels and leeks. Garnish with the reserved tarragon.

Serves 4

Note: It's a surprise when you cut into these chicken breasts and discover a delicious filling of sun-dried tomatoes. The rich sauce and baby leeks are perfect accompaniments.

Oven temperature 200°C, 400°F, Gas 6

Balsamic Duck Breasts with Potato Rösti

Preparation 10 mins **Cooking** 20 mins + 5 mins resting **Calories** 460 **Fat** 7g

2 tbsps balsamic vinegar
1 tsp clear honey
1 clove garlic, crushed
pinch of Chinese 5-spice powder
salt and black pepper
4 boneless duck breasts, about 170g each
455g waxy potatoes, peeled and grated
2 tbsps butter
2 tbsps olive oil
4 tbsps apple and plum chutney to serve
fresh herbs, such as marjoram or basil, to garnish

1   Combine the vinegar, honey, garlic, Chinese 5-spice, salt and pepper in a bowl. Cut several slashes in each duck breast with a sharp knife and rub in the mixture. Set aside.

2   Rinse the potatoes, squeeze dry in a clean tea towel, then season. Heat the butter and the oil in a frying pan, add 4 tablespoons of the potato mixture (about half) and press down gently to make 4 rösti (potato cakes). Fry for 5–6 minutes each side, until browned and cooked through. Repeat to make 4 more.

3   Meanwhile, preheat the grill to high. Cook the duck close to the heat for 3–4 minutes each side, until charred. Wrap in foil and leave to rest for 5 minutes, then slice it and serve with any juices, the rösti, and spoonfuls of the chutney. Garnish with the fresh herbs.

Serves 4

Note: A sweet-and-sour apple and plum chutney cuts through the richness of the duck, and the crispy potato pancakes help to bring all the intense flavours together.

Quick Sausage Sizzle

Preparation 6 mins **Cooking** 12 mins **Calories** 900 **Fat** 11g

1.8 kg pork or beef sausages
910g onions, thinly sliced
3 tbsps olive oil

Honey and Chilli Marinade
¼ cup red wine
½ cup honey
¼ tsp ground chilli

1   To make the marinade, mix all the ingredients together.

2   Place the sausages in a large saucepan and cover with cold water. Heat slowly until simmering point is reached, then simmer for 5 minutes. Drain well. Refrigerate until needed.

3   Heat the barbecue until hot and grease the grill bars with oil. Pour the honey and chilli marinade into a heatproof bowl and place at the side of the barbecue. Arrange the sausages from left to right on the grill or hotplate and brush with the marinade. Turn and brush with marinade after 1 minute and continue turning and basting for 10 minutes until the sausages are well glazed and cooked through. Give a final brushing with the marinade remove them to a serving platter.

4   Oil the hot plate and place on the onions. Toss at intervals and drizzle with a little oil as they cook. Serve the sausages with the onions and accompany with salad and garlic bread.

Serves 4

Note: This method is suitable for cooking a large number of sausages to serve around. Pork or beef thick sausages are used, which are simmered in water before placing on the barbecue. This prevents them from splitting and reduces cooking time. Calculate the number of sausages you need for the number of people to be served.

Lamb Noisettes with Mustard and Rosemary

Preparation 5 mins **Cooking** 10 mins **Calories** 140 **Fat** 7g

4 tbsps wholegrain mustard
2 tbsps finely chopped rosemary leaves
½ tsp minced garlic
4 lamb noisettes

1 Combine mustard, rosemary leaves and garlic. Spread mustard mixture over both sides of the noisettes. Place under a preheated grill and cook for 5 minutes each side or until cooked as desired.

Serves 4

Serving suggestion: Crusty bread with boiled or steamed baby carrots and broccoli are easy accompaniments for this tasty main meal.

Cook's tip: A noisette is a small round steak, usually of lamb. The word means 'hazelnut' in French, signifying the roundness and meatiness of the particular cut. Because the cut is so tender, it cooks very quickly.

Cajun Chops

Preparation 10 mins **Cooking** 8 mins + 10 mins standing **Calories** 696 **Fat** 28g

6 tbsps butter
3 tsps Cajun seasoning
1 small red chilli, seeded and chopped
12 lamb chops
1 tbsp olive oil

1 Beat the butter to soften it and mix in 1 1/2 teaspoons of the Cajun seasoning and all the chilli. Place the butter along the centre of a piece of plastic wrap or greaseproof paper to 1cm thickness. Fold the plastic wrap over the butter then roll it up. Smooth into a sausage shape and twist the ends. Refrigerate to firm.

2 Trim the chops if necessary and snip the membrane at the side to prevent curling. Flatten them slightly with the side of a meat mallet. Mix 1 1/2 teaspoons of the Cajun seasoning with the olive oil then rub the mixture well into both sides of the chops. Place them in a single layer onto a tray, cover and let stand for 20 minutes at room temperature, or longer in the refrigerator.

3 Heat the barbecue or electric grill to high. Place a sheet of baking paper on the grill bars, making a few slashes between the bars for ventilation. Place the chops on the grill and cook for 3 minutes each side for medium or 4 minutes for well-done. When cooked, transfer to a serving plate and top each chop with a round slice of Cajun butter.

Serves 3–4

Teriyaki Tenderloins

Preparation 5 mins + marinating time **Cooking** 5 mins **Calories** 181 **Fat** trace

455g chicken tenderloins

Teriyaki Marinade
$\frac{1}{2}$ cup soy sauce
2 tbsps brown sugar
$\frac{1}{2}$ tsp ground ginger
2 tbsps wine vinegar
1 clove garlic, crushed
2 tbsps tomato sauce

1 To make the marinade, mix all ingredients together.

2 Place the tenderloins in a non-metallic container and stir in about half a cup of teriyaki marinade. Cover and marinate for 30 minutes at room temperature or place in the refrigerator for several hours or overnight.

3 Heat the barbecue until hot. Place a sheet of baking paper over the grill bars and make a few slits between the bars for ventilation, or place baking paper on the hot plate. Place the tenderloins on grill and cook for 2 minutes each side until cooked through and golden, brushing with marinade as they cook.

Serves 2–4

Serving Suggestions

A Serve with steamed rice and vegetables.

B Toss into salad greens to make a hot salad. Dress the salad with 1 tablespoon of teriyaki marinade, 1 tablespoon of vinegar and 3 tablespoons of salad oil.

C Stuff into heated pocket breads along with shredded lettuce, cucumber and onion rings and drizzle with an extra spoonful of the teriyaki marinade.

Chicken Patties Served on Basil Flapjacks with Chilli Yoghurt Sauce

Preparation 30 mins **Cooking** 5 mins + 20 mins resting **Calories** 240 **Fat** 2g

Patties

455g ground chicken meat

$1/2$ tsp salt

$1/4$ tsp pepper

1 tsp crushed garlic

$1/2$ tsp fresh chilli, chopped or chilli powder

2 tbsp dried breadcrumbs

$1/4$ cup water

Flapjacks

1 cup all-purpose flour

$1/4$ tsp baking powder

$1/4$ tsp salt

2 tbsps chopped basil

1 tsp crushed garlic

$3/4$ cup milk

1 egg

Chilli Yoghurt Sauce

1 cup natural yoghurt

2 tsps sweet chilli sauce

or to taste

1   Mix all the patty ingredients together and knead a little with 1 hand to distribute ingredients and make it fine in texture. Cover and rest in refrigerator for 20 minutes. With wet hands, form into small flat patties about 2cm in diameter. Place on a flat tray until needed and refrigerate.

2   To prepare the flapjack batter, sift the flour, baking powder and salt into a bowl. In a separate bowl, mix together the blended basil, garlic and milk, then beat in the egg. Make a well in the centre of the flour and pour in the milk mixture. Stir to form a smooth batter. Cover and set aside for 20 minutes.

3   Heat the barbecue until hot and oil the grill bars and hotplate. Brush the patties with a little oil and place them on the grill bars. Grill for 2 minutes each side.

4   Cook the flapjacks at the same time, pouring $1/4$ cup of the mixture onto the greased hotplate. Cook until bubbles appear over the surface and the bottom is golden. Flip over with an eggslice and cook until golden. Transfer to a clean towel and cover to keep hot. Repeat.

5   Serve a flapjack on each plate and arrange 3 patties on top.

6   To make the chilli yoghurt sauce, mix both ingredients together well and then place a dollop of sauce on top of the patties. Serve with a side salad and the extra flapjacks.

Serves 6

Chops in Mushroom Sauce

Preparation 10 mins **Cooking** 15 mins **Calories** 166 **Fat** 9g

45g butter
8 thick pork chops
½ tsp minced garlic
375g button mushrooms, sliced
10 spring onions, chopped
185mL white wine
1 tbsp caster sugar
1 tbsp chopped fresh parsley
freshly ground black pepper

1 Melt butter in a large frying pan and cook chops over a medium heat for 3–4 minutes each side or until tender and golden. Remove from pan and set aside, keeping the chops warm.

2 Add garlic, mushrooms and spring onions to pan and cook for 1 minute. Stir in wine and sugar, bring to the boil, then reduce heat and simmer until reduced by half. Stir in parsley and black pepper to taste. Spoon sauce over chops and serve immediately.

Serves 4

Cook's tip: When preparing mushrooms, do not peel as the skin contains much of the flavour and nutrients. It also helps the mushrooms to retain their shape during cooking and reduces the darkening of the dish. Just wipe mushrooms with a clean, damp cloth. Store mushrooms in a paper bag or cardboard box in the refrigerator. Do not store in plastic bags as this causes them to sweat.

Hot Dogs with Mustard Relish

Preparation 1 mins **Cooking** 12 mins **Calories** 370 each **Fat** 9g

12 frankfurters or thin sausages
1 cup barbecue sauce
12 hot-dog rolls
mild mustard for serving
gherkin relish or tomato pickles
to serve

1 Heat the barbecue and oil the grill bars. Place the frankfurters or sausages and turn to heat on the grill evenly, so the skin doesn't burst. Cook for 10–12 minutes, brushing with a little barbecue sauce as they're turned. Turn down the heat or push them to a cooler part of the barbecue if they cook too quickly.

2 Split the rolls, keeping the 2 halves attached and place the cut side down on the hot plate to toast.

3 Fill each roll with a frankfurter or sausage, squeeze a row of mustard along the side and spoon in the gherkin relish or tomato pickles.

Makes 12

Perfect Sirloin Steak

Preparation 5 mins + 15 mins marinating time **Cooking** 5–15 mins **Calories** 344 **Fat** 10g

4 sirloin steaks
2 tsps crushed garlic
2 tsp oil
salt and black pepper

Garlic Butter
4 tbsp butter
1 tsp crushed garlic
1 tbsp parsley flakes
2 tsps lemon juice

1   Bring the steaks to room temperature. Mix the garlic, oil and salt and pepper together. Rub onto both sides of the steak. Stand for 10–15 minutes at room temperature.

2   Heat the barbecue until hot and oil the grill bars. Arrange the steaks and sear for 1 minute each side. Move the steaks to a cooler part of the barbecue and continue cooking over a moderate heat or turn the heat down. If the heat can't be reduced, elevate the steaks on a wire cakerack placed on the grill bars. Cook 5–6 minutes for rare, 7–10 minutes for medium and 10–14 minutes for well done. Turn during cooking.

3   To make garlic butter, mix all ingredients together

4   Serve the remaining garlic butter in a small pot with a spoon.

Serves 4

Apricot Steaks

Preparation 15 mins **Cooking** 15 mins **Calories** 165 **Fat** 9g

4 scotch fillet or rib eye steaks
black pepper
oil or butter for cooking
1 small onion, chopped
425g canned unsweetened apricots
2 tsps tomato paste
2 tsps mango chutney

1 Trim steaks and season with pepper.

2 Heat oil or butter in a large frying pan on high heat. Add steaks, cook for about 40 seconds and then quickly turn, retain high heat for 30 seconds then turn heat down to medium and cook for 3 minutes. Turn meat once more and cook for 3–4 minutes until meat is cooked as desired. Remove to a plate and keep warm.

3 Add onion to pan and cook for 2 minutes. Drain apricots and reserve the juice. To the pan add, quarter cup of apricot juice, the tomato paste and the mango chutney, stir to combine. Spoon in the apricots and heat through. Add extra juice if needed.

4 Place steaks onto a heated serving platter and cover with sauce. Serve with buttered noodles and a salad.

Serves 4

Chicken Satay Skewers

Preparation 15 mins + 1 hr standing time **Cooking** 20 mins **Calories** 295 **Fat** 22g

500g chicken thigh fillets

Satay Sauce Marinade
¹/₂ cup peanut butter
¹/₂ cup water
1 clove garlic, crushed
1 tbsp brown sugar
pinch chilli powder or to taste
2 tsps soy sauce
1 tbsp grated onion

1 Mix all the satay sauce ingredients together in a saucepan. Heat to a simmer and simmer while stirring occasionally for 5 minutes. Allow to cool completely.

2 Soak bamboo skewers in water. Cut the thigh fillets into cubes, place in a bowl and mix in the cooled satay sauce. Cover and stand to marinate for 1 hour or longer if refrigerated.

3 Thread 4–5 cubes onto each skewer, spaced to be almost touching. Heat the grill plate or barbecue to medium high and cover with a sheet of baking paper. Place the skewers on the paper and cook for 12–15 minutes, turning and brushing frequently with the remaining satay sauce. Increase the heat for the last 3–5 minutes to brown and cook through. Serve immediately.

Serves 4

Note: For party finger food, thread 3 cubes onto small skewers. Small skewers may also be pan grilled.

Lebanese Lamb Rolls

Preparation 20 mins **Cooking** 20 mins **Calories** 165 **Fat** 10g

2 tbsps oil
1 onion, chopped
500g minced lamb
1 small eggplant, cubed
2 tsps ground allspice
1 tsp chilli sauce
3 tbsps red wine
440g canned tomatoes, undrained and mashed
4 tbsps sultanas
3 tbsps pine nuts, toasted
4 large pita bread rounds
4 lettuce leaves, shredded
1 carrot, peeled and grated

1 Preheat the oven. Heat oil in a large frying pan and cook onion for 3–4 minutes or until softened. Add lamb and cook over a medium–high heat for 5 minutes longer or until brown. Stir in eggplant, allspice, chilli sauce, wine, tomatoes and sultanas. Bring to the boil, then reduce heat and simmer for 5 minutes, or until sauce has reduced and thickened slightly. Stir in pine nuts.

2 Heat pita breads in the oven for 5 minutes or until heated through but not crisp. Spread with lamb mixture, top with lettuce and carrot, and roll up. Serve immediately.

Serves 4

Oven temperature 180°C, 350°F, Gas 4

Fish and Shellfish

Many people may think seafood is out of the question if they're pressed for time but our expert team has worked hard to ensure you can enjoy this little luxury without spending hours in the kitchen. Take a bite into our shellfish and rocket pizza, make a meal of our monkfish and prosciutto or feast on our Parmesan-crusted fish and you'll never order take-away again! Whether for a family meal or for hosting guests, keep these recipes handy – we know you'll visit them time and time again.

Marinated Grilled Fish with Basil Tomato Topping

Preparation 10 mins + 2 hrs marinating **Cooking** 4 mins **Calories** 125 **Fat** 6g

4 x 200g white fish fillets

Marinade
1 tbsp grated onion
2 tbsps olive oil
2 tbsps lemon juice
$1/4$ tsp ground black pepper
$1/2$ tsp salt or pepper, to taste
3 bay leaves

Topping
10 basil leaves
2 Roma tomatoes, sliced
1 tbsp grated parmesan cheese

1 Place the fish in a single layer in a non-metallic dish. Mix together the marinade ingredients and pour over the fish. Cover and marinate for 2 hours in the refrigerator.

2 Remove the fish from the marinade. Preheat the grill, cover with baking paper and place the fish on top. Close the grill and cook for 3 minutes or according to thickness, until the fish just flakes. Open the grill, place 3 basil leaves on top. Cover with 2–3 slices of tomato and top the tomato with cheese. Cover with a sheet of baking paper, close the lid and cook for 30–40 seconds. Remove immediately to heated plates and serve with desired accompaniments.

Serves 3–4

Monkfish and Prosciutto with Braised Capsicums

Preparation 10 mins **Cooking** 25 mins **Calories** 303 **Fat** 4g

3 tbsps extra virgin olive oil

4 large red, green, orange, or yellow capsicums deseeded and thickly sliced

4 cloves garlic, chopped

2 sprigs fresh thyme

salt and black pepper

4 monkfish fillets, about 225g each

4 slices prosciutto

2 tbsps balsamic vinegar

chopped basil leaves to garnish

1 Heat 2 tablespoons of the oil in a large heavy-based saucepan, then add the capsicums, garlic, thyme, 2 tablespoons of water and the seasoning. Cook, partially covered, for 20 minutes or until softened and browned, stirring occasionally.

2 Meanwhile, season the monkfish well, then wrap a slice of prosciutto around each fillet. Secure the prosciutto with a wetted cocktail stick. Heat the remaining oil in a large heavy-based frying pan, add the fillets and fry for 8–10 minutes, turning once, until browned and cooked through. Cover loosely with foil and set aside.

3 Add the vinegar to the capsicums in the pan and cook for 5 minutes to warm through. Remove the cocktail sticks from the monkfish and prosciutto, then cut the monkfish into thick slices and garnish with the basil. Serve with the capsicums and pan juices.

Serves 4

Note: Delicately flavoured monkfish wrapped in prosciutto is a wonderfully luxurious combination. For a really pretty dish, choose different-coloured capsicums.

Grilled Tuna in Vegetables

Preparation 12 mins **Cooking** 5 mins **Calories** 125 **Fat** 9g

3 tbsps olive oil

2 tbsps balsamic or red-wine vinegar

1 tbsp chopped basil leaves

freshly ground black pepper

4 baby eggplants, halved

4 plums (egg or Italian) tomatoes, halved

1 leek, cut into 7½cm pieces and halved

4 tuna steaks

1 Place oil, vinegar, basil and black pepper to taste in a bowl and whisk to combine. Brush eggplant, tomatoes, leek and tuna with the vinegar mixture.

2 Heat a lightly oiled char-grill or frying pan over a high heat, add vegetables and tuna and cook, brushing frequently with remaining vinegar mixture, for 2 minutes each side or until vegetables and tuna are cooked. To serve, arrange vegetables and tuna on serving plates and serve immediately.

Note: When cooking fresh tuna take care not to overcook it. The experts recommend that you cook tuna so that it is still pink inside. If tuna is unavailable this recipe can also be made using swordfish or salmon.

Serves 4

Parmesan-Crusted Fish

Preparation 25 mins **Cooking** 10 mins **Calories** 345 **Fat** 16g

4 firm white fish fillets
½ cup plain flour
1 tsp paprika
freshly ground pepper
1 cup dried breadcrumbs
90g grated Parmesan cheese
1 egg, lightly beaten
2 tbsps olive oil

Lemon Thyme Butter
60g butter
1 tbsp grated lemon rind
1 tbsp lemon juice
1 tbsp chopped fresh thyme or lemon
thyme

1   Pat fish dry. Combine flour, paprika and black pepper to taste. Combine breadcrumbs and Parmesan cheese. Coat fillets with flour mixture. Dip in egg, then coat with breadcrumb mixture. Heat oil in a frying pan over a medium heat, add fillets and cook for 2–3 minutes each side or until cooked.

2   To make the lemon thyme butter, heat butter, lemon rind, lemon juice and thyme in a saucepan over a medium heat for 1 minute or until butter melts. Serve with fish fillets.

Serving suggestion: Accompany with potato crisps and vegetables. Make the crisps using a vegetable peeler and peeling thin slices from potatoes. Dry slices and deep-fry for 7–10 minutes or until cooked. Drain and sprinkle with salt.

Note: When buying fish fillets, look for those that are shiny and firm with a pleasant sea smell. Avoid fillets that are dull, soft, discoloured or 'ooze' water when touched.

Serves 4

Shellfish and Rocket Pizzas

Preparation 10 mins **Cooking** 15 mins **Calories** 635 **Fat** 8g

24 whole raw peeled tiger prawns, defrosted if frozen

2 tbsp olive oil

2 cloves garlic, crushed

12 small prepared squid tubes, cut into rings

2 x 23cm pizza bases

2 tbsp sun-dried tomato purée

16 anchovy fillets in oil, drained and chopped

1³⁄4 cups mozzarella cheese, grated

¹⁄2 cup rocket

Parmesan cheese to serve (optional)

1 Preheat the oven. Put 2 large baking trays into the oven to heat.

2 Rinse the prawns and pat dry with kitchen towels. Heat the oil in a large heavy-based frying pan, add the garlic, prawns and squid and stir-fry for 3 minutes, or until the prawns turn pink and the squid is opaque.

3 Spread the pizza bases with the tomato purée and top with the cooked seafood, anchovies and mozzarella. Place on the heated baking trays and cook for 10–12 minutes, until the cheese is golden, swapping shelves halfway through. Scatter the rocket over the pizzas and shave over the Parmesan (if using) with a vegetable peeler.

Serves 4

Note: Anyone who likes good food will love this shellfish and rocket pizza. If you're cooking for 2, halve the quantities and reduce the cooking time by a couple of minutes.

Oven temperature 220°C, 440°F, Gas 7

Spaghetti Vongole

Preparation 10 mins **Cooking** 25 mins **Calories** 460 **Fat** 2g

290g spaghetti
3 tbsps virgin olive oil
1 onion, very finely chopped
2 garlic cloves, finely chopped
455g vongoles (clams) cleaned
and sandless
½ cup white wine
salt and black pepper
1 tbsp fresh chopped oregano

1 Cook the spaghetti in boiling water, refresh in cold water, then stir with half the oil and set aside.

2 Heat the remaining oil in a large cooking pot over a high heat. Add the onion and garlic and cook for 1 minute.

3 Add vongoles, wine, salt and pepper.

4 When all the clams have opened (discard any that don't open after 10 minutes), add the spaghetti and oregano. Cook for another 2 minutes and serve.

Serves 3–4

Gratin of Scallops and Mushrooms

Preparation 10 mins **Cooking** 10 mins **Calories** 175 **Fat** 14g

4 large fresh scallops
145mL milk
145mL double cream
30g plain flour
30g butter
¼ tsp freshly grated nutmeg
55g Gruyère or Lancashire cheese, diced
115g button mushroooms trimmed and halved
2 tbsps butter, extra

1 Trim the scallops, remove the orange coral and cut the white flesh of each scallop into 8 pieces.

2 Pour the milk into a non-stick saucepan. Add the scallops (except for the corals), bring to the boil and simmer for 5 minutes. Remove the scallops from the milk and set aside.

3 Add the cream, flour, butter, and nutmeg to the milk and whisk gently over a low heat until the sauce thickens. Add the cheese and allow to melt without letting it boil.

4 Sauté mushrooms in the extra butter for 2–3 minutes.

5 Spoon some scallops onto the centre of each serving plate. Arrange mushrooms around the scallops. Drizzle any juices over the mushrooms.

6 Top scallop pieces with corals and cover with the sauce.

Serves 4

Swordfish with Coriander Butter

Preparation 6 mins **Cooking** 10 mins **Calories** 423 **Fat** 16g

½ cup sweet butter

2 tbsps finely chopped coriander leaves

1 tbsp grated Parmesan cheese

4 swordfish steaks

1 tbsp olive oil

4 zucchinis, cut into long slices

1 red capsicum, quartered

1 Cream the butter until soft and mix in the coriander and Parmesan. Pile into a butter pot and set aside.

2 Heat the barbecue grill until hot and brush with oil. Brush the fish steaks with oil, place on the grill bars and cook for 3–4 minutes each side according to thickness. Brush or spray vegetables with oil and place on the grill. Cook for a few minutes on each side. Remove the fish steaks and vegetables to heated plates. Top each swordfish steak with a generous dollop of the coriander butter and serve immediately.

Serves 4

Salmon with Pineapple Salsa

Preparation 6 mins **Cooking** 10 mins **Calories** 344 **Fat** 3g

4 salmon chops

Pineapple Salsa
1 cup canned crushed pineapple, drained
2 green onions, chopped
1 fresh red chilli, chopped
1 tbsp lemon juice
2 tbsps chopped mint leaves

1 Cook the salmon on a lightly oiled preheated barbecue or under a grill for 3–5 minutes each side (or until cooked).
2 To make the salsa, combine all the ingredients. Serve with the salmon.

Serves 4

Seafood and Noodle Stir-fry

Preparation 20 mins **Cooking** 5 mins **Calories** 464 **Fat** 3g

2 tbsps sesame oil
1 clove garlic, crushed
2 small red chillies, chopped
1 tbsp grated fresh ginger
900g prepared mixed seafood
$\frac{1}{2}$ red capsicum, sliced
$\frac{1}{2}$ cup snowpeas, cut into
2$\frac{1}{}$cm pieces
225g asparagus spears, cut into
2.5cm pieces
1 tbsp shredded basil leaves
340g egg noodles, cooked
1 tbsp cornflour
$\frac{1}{4}$ cup hoisin sauce
$\frac{1}{2}$ cup water
2 tbsps sesame seeds, toasted

1 Heat the oil in a wok. Add the garlic, chilli and ginger. Stir-fry for 1 minute. Add the seafood, capsicum, snowpeas, asparagus and basil. Stir-fry until the seafood is just cooked. Add the noodles. Stir-fry for 1–2 minutes.

2 Combine the cornflour, hoisin sauce and water. Stir into the pan. Cook, stirring, until the sauce boils and thickens. Sprinkle with the sesame seeds and serve.

Serves 4

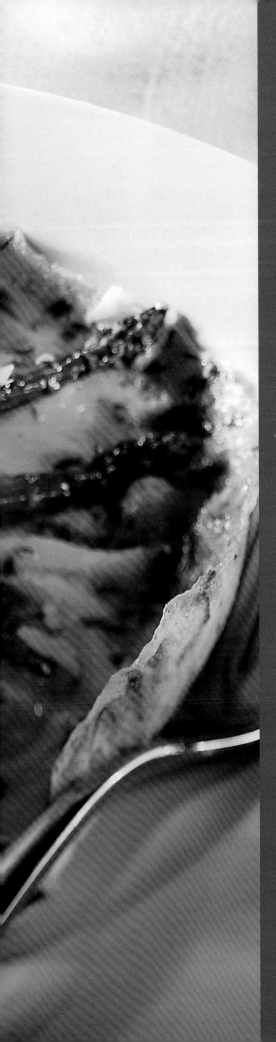

Vegetable Dishes

Depart from the dull with a refreshing range of recipes that make the most of everyday vegetables. While every family has its favourites, from the humble baked potato to buttered beans, it's comforting to know you can tempt the tastebuds with a variety of new ideas. Try your hand at our feta and ricotta – stuffed tomatoes or our creamy polenta, spinach and cheese bake. They're delicious, nutritious and simple to prepare. A trip to your green grocer will open up a whole new world of possibilities. If only everything in life were this easy…

Asparagus, Ricotta and Herb Frittata

Preparation 10 mins **Cooking** 20 mins **Calories** 430 **Fat** 8g

455g fresh asparagus
12 medium eggs
2 small cloves garlic, crushed
4 tbsps chopped fresh mixed herbs, including basil, chives and parsley
salt and black pepper
4 tbsps butter
100g ricotta cheese
squeeze of lemon juice
olive or truffle oil to drizzle
Parmesan cheese to serve
fresh chives to garnish

1 Preheat the grill to high. Place the asparagus in a grill pan and grill for 10 minutes or until charred and tender, turning once. Keep warm.

2 Meanwhile, whisk together the eggs, garlic, herbs and seasoning. Melt 2 tablespoons of the butter in an ovenproof frying pan until it starts to foam, then immediately pour in a quarter of the egg mixture and cook for 1–2 minutes until almost set.

3 Place under the preheated grill for 3–4 minutes, until the egg is cooked through and the top of the frittata is set, then transfer to a plate. Keep warm while you make the 3 remaining frittatas, adding more butter when necessary.

4 Arrange a quarter of the asparagus and a quarter of the ricotta over each frittata, squeeze over the lemon juice, season and drizzle with oil. Top with shavings of the Parmesan, garnish with the fresh chives and serve.

Serves 4

Note: Grilling the asparagus brings extra texture and flavour to this Italian-style frittata and the creamy ricotta adds the finishing touch. Serve with warmed crusty ciabatta.

54

Fettuccine Carbonara

Preparation 10 mins **Cooking** 15 mins **Calories** 240 **Fat** 12g

500g fettuccine

Carbonara Sauce
250g ham, prosciutto or bacon, chopped
$1/2$ cup chicken stock
1 cup double cream
7 eggs, lightly beaten
2 tbsps chopped flat-leaf parsley
freshly ground black pepper

1 Cook pasta in boiling water in a large saucepan following packet directions. Drain, set aside and keep warm.

2 To make sauce, cook ham, prosciutto or bacon in a frying pan over a medium heat for 3 minutes or until crisp.

3 Stir in stock and cream, bring to simmering and simmer until sauce is reduced by half.

4 Remove pan from heat, whisk in eggs, parsley and black pepper to taste. Return pan to heat and cook, stirring, for 1 minute. Remove pan from heat, add hot pasta to sauce and toss to combine. Serve immediately.

Serves 6

Roman Kebabs

Preparation 10 mins **Cooking** 8 mins **Calories** 597 **Fat** 10g

1 French baguette
455g mozzarella cheese
4 tomatoes
5 tbsps olive oil
1 tbsp lemon juice
1 tsp dried oregano
salt and black pepper
fresh basil to garnish

1. Preheat the oven. Soak 4 wooden skewers in water for 10 minutes.

2. Cut the bread into 16 x 1cm-thick slices, and cut the mozzarella into 12 slices. Slice each tomato into 3, discarding the ends.

3. Combine the oil, lemon juice, oregano and seasoning in a shallow dish. Generously brush both sides of the bread with the oil, then thread the bread onto the skewers, alternating with the mozzarella and tomato slices and finishing with bread. Pour over any of the remaining oil mixture.

4. Place the kebabs on a baking sheet and cook for 6–8 minutes, carefully turning over halfway through, until the bread is crisp and the cheese is just starting to melt. Cool slightly before serving and garnish with the fresh basil.

Serves 4

Oven temperature 230°C, 450°F, Gas 8

Creamy Polenta, Spinach and Cheese Bake

Preparation 10 mins **Cooking** 25 mins **Calories** 463 **Fat** 8g

1 tbsp olive oil

1 small onion, finely chopped

2 cloves garlic, crushed

1/2 tsp ground coriander

455g fresh spinach

1 1/4 cups light cream

1/2 cup gorgonzola cheese, crumbled

pinch of ground nutmeg

salt and black pepper

455g ready-made polenta, thinly sliced

1 mozzarella cheese ball (about 145g), thinly sliced

1 Preheat the oven. Heat the oil in a saucepan and gently fry the onion, garlic and coriander for 5 minutes, or until the onion is softened.

2 Blanch the spinach in boiling salted water for 1 minute, refresh under cold running water, then drain well and squeeze out any excess moisture. Stir the spinach into the pan with the cream, gorgonzola, nutmeg, salt and pepper. Bring to a simmer, then transfer to a large, shallow, ovenproof dish.

3 Arrange the polenta and mozzarella slices over the top of the spinach mixture, pressing down well. Bake for 15 minutes or until bubbling. Preheat the grill to high. Place the bake under the grill for 1–2 minutes, until browned.

Serves 4

Note: Bubbling mozzarella covers ready-made polenta and a bed of creamy spinach in this great-tasting vegetarian supper dish. Serve it with a green salad.

Oven temperature 230°C, 450°F, Gas 8

Spinach, Olive and Feta Frittata

Preparation 15 mins **Cooking** 25 mins **Calories** 616 **Fat** 8g

10 eggs, lightly beaten
1 tbsp fresh oregano, chopped
freshly ground black pepper
5 tbsps olive oil
225g potatoes, peeled and diced
1 brown onion, diced
1 clove garlic, crushed
2 cups baby spinach
4 tbsps pitted kalamata olives, halved
1/2 cup feta cheese, crumbled
1/2 cup semi-dried tomatoes
3 large red capsicums

1. Combine the eggs and oregano in a bowl, season with black pepper and set aside.

2. Heat the oil in a 23cm pan and sauté the potatoes, onion and garlic for a few minutes until soft.

3. Add the spinach and cook until it begins to wilt. Remove the pan from the heat, then add the olives, feta and semi-dried tomatoes.

4. Return the pan to a very low heat, pour in the egg mixture and cook for 10–15 minutes. Run a spatula around the sides of the pan as the frittata is cooking and tilt it slightly so that the egg mixture runs down the sides a little.

5. Meanwhile make the capsicum sauce. Halve the capsicums and remove the seeds. Chargrill the capsicums until black under a griller. Let them cool and remove the skins. Place into a food processor and process until puréed. Transfer to a bowl. Makes 1 cup.

6. When the frittata is almost done through the middle, place it under a grill for 5 minutes to cook and brown the top.

7. Serve in wedges with the roasted capsicum sauce.

Serves 4

Feta and Ricotta Stuffed Tomatoes

Preparation 5 mins **Cooking** 25 mins **Calories** 198 **Fat** 6g

6 large firm tomatoes
1 cup feta cheese, crumbed
1 cup ricotta cheese
4 tbsps pine nuts, chopped
10 black olives, pitted and chopped
1½ tbsps fresh oregano, chopped
3 tbsps whole-wheat breadcrumbs
freshly ground black pepper
6 black olives, to garnish
oregano leaves

1 Preheat the oven. Cut the top quarters off each tomato and scoop the centres into a bowl. Reserve the tops of the tomatoes. Combine half the tomato mixture with the feta, ricotta, pine nuts, olives, oregano, breadcrumbs and pepper. Beat the mixture together and spoon it back into the tomato cases (piling the tops high). Replace the tops on each tomato.

2 Place in a shallow oven-proof dish and bake for 20–25 minutes.

3 Garnish with an olive and the oregano to serve.

Serves 6

Oven temperature 180°C, 350°F, Gas 4

Deep-Fried Okra

Preparation 8 mins **Cooking** 2 mins **Calories** 283 **Fat** 2g

225g okra
1 egg
1 cup plain flour
1 cup ice-cold water
oil, for frying

Garlic Walnut Sauce
2 slices bread
1/2 cup water
1/2 cup walnuts
2 cloves garlic, roughly chopped
2 tbsps white-wine vinegar
1 tbsp olive oil
salt and black pepper to taste

1 To make the garlic walnut sauce, soak the bread in water for 5 minutes. Squeeze out the water. Place the walnuts in food processor, and process until finely chopped. Add the bread, garlic and vinegar. Process until combined. While the motor is running, add the olive oil, salt and pepper and process until a paste is formed.

2 Wash and trim the okra. In a large bowl, whisk the egg until frothy, add the flour and water and whisk together until the batter is also frothy.

3 Heat the oil in a large frying pan, dip the okra in the batter and cook in the oil for 1–2 minutes or until lightly brown.

4 Drain on absorbent paper and serve with the lemon wedges and the garlic walnut sauce.

Serves 4

Note: The garlic walnut sauce goes equally well with chicken, fish or vegetables.

Eggplant Rolls

Preparation 8 mins **Cooking** 25 mins **Calories** 384 **Fat** 7g

2 eggplants (about 225g each)
3 tbsps olive oil
3 medium tomatoes, seeded and diced
1 cup mozzarella cheese, finely diced
2 tbsps basil leaves, chopped
salt and freshly ground black pepper
extra basil leaves, for serving

Dressing
4 tbsps olive oil
1 tomato, diced
1 tbsp balsamic vinegar
2 tbsps pine nuts, toasted
salt and black pepper

1 Remove the stalks from the eggplants and slice them lengthwise in 5mm sections. Brush the slices on both sides with oil and grill both sides until soft and beginning to brown.

2 Preheat the oven. In a bowl, combine together the tomatoes, mozzarella, basil and seasoning. Spoon a little onto the end of each slice of eggplant and roll up. Place it seam-side down in a greased oven-proof dish and bake for 15–17 minutes.

3 Meanwhile, make the dressing/olive oil in a small pan, using a little of the dressing oil, sauté the tomato until softened. Add the remaining oil, vinegar and pine nuts, and gently warm. Season to taste. Arrange the eggplant rolls on a platter and spoon the dressing over them.

4 Garnish with the fresh basil leaves to serve.

Serves 4

Oven temperature 180°C, 350°F, Gas 4

Asparagus and Lemon Risotto

Preparation 15 mins **Cooking** 25 mins **Calories** 363 **Fat** 3g

2 tbsps olive oil
1 onion, chopped
2 cups arborio rice
1 cup white wine
3 cups chicken or vegetable stock
1 cup asparagus tips, cut into bite-sized pieces
4 tbsps butter
½ cup Parmesan cheese, grated
salt and black pepper
2 tbsps chopped fresh parsley
finely grated zest of 1 lemon

1 Heat the oil in a large, heavy-based saucepan or frying pan, then add the onion and fry for 3–4 minutes, until golden. Add the rice and stir for 1 minute or until coated with the oil. Stir in the wine and bring to the boil, then reduce the heat and continue stirring for 4–5 minutes, until the wine has been absorbed by the rice.

2 Pour about a third of the stock into the rice and simmer for 4–5 minutes, stirring constantly. Once the stock has been absorbed, add half the remaining stock and cook, stirring, until absorbed. Add the remaining stock and the asparagus and cook, stirring, for 5 minutes or until the rice and asparagus are tender but still firm to the bite.

3 Add the butter and half the Parmesan and season. Cook for 1 minute, or until the butter and cheese have melted into the rice, stirring constantly. Sprinkle with the remaining Parmesan and the parsley and lemon zest.

Serves 6

Note: Rich, creamy, and full of flavour, this fabulous risotto is very easy to make. Be sure not to overcook it; each grain of rice should keep its shape and firmness.

Pumpkin with Lemon and Cheese

Preparation 15 mins **Cooking** 20 mins **Calories** 127 **Fat** 8g

680g pumpkin or squash, peeled, seeded and cut into chunks

1 cup chicken or vegetable stock

2 tsps arrowroot

juice of 1 lemon

grated zest of $\frac{1}{2}$ a lemon

1 cup aged Cheddar cheese, grated

2 tbsps chopped fresh dill or parsley

salt and black pepper

1 Place the pumpkin or squash in a steamer or a metal colander covered with foil. Set over a saucepan of simmering water and steam for 5–10 minutes, until tender but still firm.

2 Meanwhile, bring the stock to the boil in a small saucepan. Mix the arrowroot with the lemon juice until smooth, then stir in the lemon zest and add to the boiling stock. Simmer, stirring constantly, for 1–2 minutes, until the sauce thickens and looks glossy. Add $\frac{1}{2}$ the Cheddar and simmer for a further 1–2 minutes, until the cheese has melted. Stir in the dill or parsley, season and mix well.

3 Preheat the grill to high. Transfer the pumpkin to a flameproof dish, cover with the lemon sauce and sprinkle with the remaining Cheddar. Place under the grill and cook for 5–8 minutes, until the sauce is bubbling and golden.

Serves 6

Desserts and Sweet Things

Take a trip to seventh heaven with this delectable range of dishes. Never before has it been so easy to make up a dessert that's totally satisfying and requires so little fuss. Sink your teeth into our shaggy dog lamingtons, or plunge your fork into our peach and hazelnut crumble and you'll know that the best-loved course on the dinner menu need not be just ice cream.

Mini Chocolate Muffins with Mocha Sauce

Preparation 10 mins + 5 mins cooling **Cooking** 15 mins **Calories** 160 each **Fat** 11g each

4 tbsps butter, diced, plus extra for greasing

½ cup semisweet chocolate, broken into pieces

2 medium eggs

⅓ cup caster sugar

¾ cup plain flour

¼ tsp baking powder

⅕ cup cocoa powder, sifted, plus extra for dusting

Mocha Sauce

1 cup semisweet chocolate, broken into pieces

⅓ cup espresso or other strong, good quality coffee

⅝ cup double cream

1 Preheat the oven. Grease a 12-hole muffin tray. Melt the butter and chocolate in a bowl set over a saucepan of simmering water. Combine the eggs, sugar, flour, baking powder and cocoa powder into a bowl and beat for 1 minute, then beat in the melted chocolate and butter.

2 Spoon into the muffin tray, allowing 1 tablespoon for each hole. Bake for 15 minutes or until risen and firm to the touch.

3 Meanwhile, make the mocha sauce. Put the chocolate, coffee and a quarter of a cup of the cream into a small pan and heat gently. Simmer for 1–2 minutes, until the sauce has thickened slightly. Keep warm.

4 Leave the muffins to cool on a wire rack for 5 minutes. Whisk the remaining cream until thickened, then spoon over the muffins together with the mocha sauce. Serve dusted with the cocoa powder.

Makes 12

Note: You'll need a 12-hole, non-stick muffin tray for these mini muffins or, if you prefer, you can make large muffins and increase the cooking time to 25 minutes.

Oven temperature 180°C, 350°F, Gas 4

Raspberry and Elderflower Fool

Preparation 15 mins + 30 mins chilling **Calories** 371 **Fat** 36g

3 cups raspberries, defrosted if frozen,
plus extra to decorate

4 tbsps elderflower cordial

4 tbsps icing sugar, or to taste,
plus extra to dust

2 cups double cream

fresh mint to decorate

1 Purée the raspberries and cordial until smooth in a food processor or with a hand blender. Blend in the icing sugar. Spoon 1 tablespoon of the mixture into each dessert glass, reserving the remaining purée, and set aside.

2 Whisk the cream until it holds its shape, then gradually fold into the reserved raspberry purée.

3 Spoon the raspberry cream into the glasses and chill in the fridge for 30 minutes. Serve decorated with the extra raspberries and mint and dusted with the icing sugar.

Serves 6

Note: A fresh-tasting fruit fool that needs no cooking. Other fruits such as strawberries or blackberries can be used, but you may need to adjust the quantity of icing sugar.

Nutty Meringues

Preparation 8 mins **Cooking** 5 mins **Calories** 434 **Fat** 33g

4 prepared meringue cases

Marshmallow Filling
3 tbsps chopped mixed nuts
8 marshmallows, quartered
2 tbsps desiccated coconut
125mL double cream, whipped

Chocolate Sauce
125g dark chocolate
125mL double cream
1 tbsp chocolate liqueur (optional)
1 tbsp flaked almonds, toasted

1 To make filling, fold nuts, marshmallows and coconut into cream. Spoon mixture into meringue cases.

2 To make sauce, place chocolate, cream and liqueur into a small saucepan and cook, stirring, over a low heat for 5 minutes or until well combined. Drizzle sauce over meringues and spoon remaining sauce onto plates. Decorate with flaked almonds.

Serves 4

Persimmon Claude

Preparation 15 mins **Cooking** 5 mins + 4 hrs freezing **Calories** 150 **Fat** 6g

6 persimmons, well ripened
100g caster sugar
¹/₂ cup water
2 tbsps orange juice
2 tsps lemon juice
250mL cream, lightly whipped

1 Carefully remove lids of the persimmon with a sharp pointed knife. Gently remove pulp with a tiny pointed spoon, being careful not to tear the skin, and set aside. Freeze the empty shells.
2 Make a syrup by boiling the sugar and water together for 1 minute. Set aside and allow to cool.
3 Puree the persimmon pulp and mix with the cooled syrup and orange and lemon juice.
4 Fold into the lightly whipped cream. Pour mixture into frozen shells and place in the freezer for approximately 4 hours before serving.

Serves 6

Sweet Brioche with Grilled Peaches

Preparation 10 mins **Cooking** 12 mins **Calories** 420 **Fat** 24g

4 large, ripe peaches, halved and
stoned
1 tbsp clear honey
6 tbsps sweet butter
2 medium eggs, lightly beaten
2 tbsps sweet white wine
2 tbsps caster sugar
1 tbsp lemon juice
pinch of ground cinnamon
4 slices brioche
crème fraîche to serve

1 Preheat the grill to medium. Place the peach halves, cut-side
up, in a grill pan and top each with a drizzle of honey and a
knob of butter, reserving half the butter for frying. Grill for 5–6
minutes, until softened and golden.

2 Meanwhile, whisk together the eggs, wine, sugar, lemon
juice and cinnamon. Dip the slices of brioche in the egg
mixture to coat.

3 Melt the remaining butter in a large frying pan and gently fry
the brioche slices for 2–3 minutes each side, until crisp and
golden. Top each slice with 2 peach halves and their juice
and a spoonful of crème fraîche.

Serves 4

*Note: Don't worry if the peach stones won't come out easily. Simply cut
the fruit away from the stone in thick juicy slices and grill them for slightly
less time than for halves.*

Soufflé Omelette with Apricots

Preparation 20 mins **Cooking** 7 mins **Calories** 160 **Fat** 10g

4 eggs, separated
2 tbsps double cream
1 tbsp caster sugar
15g butter
3 tbsps apricot jam, warmed
440g canned apricot halves, drained
icing sugar, for dusting
double cream, whipped

1 Place egg yolks, cream and sugar in a mixing bowl and beat until combined.

2 Beat egg whites until stiff peaks form. Fold into egg yolk mixture.

3 Melt butter in a small frying pan. Spread half the egg mixture evenly over the base of the pan and cook over a low heat for 1–2 minutes, and then place pan under a preheated grill and cook until set. Spread half the omelette with half the jam and top with half the apricots. Fold, cut in half and ease onto a serving plate. Dust with icing sugar and serve with cream. Repeat with remaining egg mixture to make a second omelette.

Serves 4

Flourless Chocolate Cake

Preparation 10 mins **Cooking** 45 mins **Calories** 188 each serve **Fat** 6g each serve

6 eggs, separated
½ cup caster sugar
⅕ cup cocoa powder, sifted
1 cup bittersweet chocolate, melted

Toffee
½ cup caster sugar

1 Preheat the oven. Beat the egg yolks with the sugar until thick and creamy. Mix in the cocoa powder and chocolate. Beat the egg whites until soft peaks form. Fold into the chocolate mixture. Pour into a greased and lined 23cm springform pan. Bake for 35 minutes. Cool.

2 To make the toffee, melt the sugar in a heavy saucepan over high heat. Shake the saucepan so sugar browns evenly. Bring to a boil and cook until golden. Pour onto a sheet of greased foil and allow to set. Break into large pieces and use to decorate chocolate cake.

Serves 12–14

Oven temperature 180°C, 350°F, Gas 4

Rum Raisin Nut Brownies

Preparation 15 mins + 15 mins soaking **Cooking** 35 mins **Calories** 238 each **Fat** 7g each

½ cup raisins
¼ cup brandy
½ cup bittersweet chocolate, chopped
½ cup sweet butter
2 eggs
⅞ cup brown sugar
1 cup plain flour, sifted
1 cup macadamia or brazil nuts, chopped
caster sugar, sifted, for dusting
drinking chocolate, sifted, for dusting

1 Place the raisins and brandy in a bowl and set aside to soak for 15 minutes or until the raisins soften.

2 Preheat the oven. Place the chocolate and butter in a heatproof bowl set over a saucepan of simmering water and heat, stirring constantly, until the mixture is smooth. Remove the bowl from the pan and set aside to cool slightly.

3 Place the eggs and brown sugar in a bowl and beat until thick and creamy. Add the chocolate mixture, flour, nuts and raisin mixture and mix to combine.

4 Pour the mixture into a greased 20cm-square cake pan and bake for 35 minutes, or until firm. Cool the brownies in the pan. Then cut into squares and dust with the caster sugar and drinking chocolate.

Makes 16

Note: For a dinner party dessert, top these irresistibly rich and moist brownies with thick cream, chocolate sauce or berry coulis and decorate with fresh fruit.

Oven temperature 180°C, 350°F, Gas 4

Shaggy Dog Lamingtons

Preparation 25 mins **Cooking** 45 mins **Calories** 456 each **Fat** 17g

1 butter or sponge cake (about 18 x 28cm)

2 cups shredded coconut

1 tbsp drinking chocolate, sifted

Chocolate Cream Filling

1¼ cups double cream

1 cup bittersweet chocolate, chopped

Chocolate Icing

2 cups icing sugar

2 tbsps cocoa powder

2 tbsps butter, softened

¼ cup milk

1. Cut the cake into 5cm squares. Split each square horizontally and set aside.

2. To make the filling, place the cream and chocolate in a heatproof bowl, set over a saucepan of simmering water and heat, stirring, until the chocolate melts and the mixture is smooth. Remove the bowl from the pan and set aside to cool. Beat the filling until light and fluffy.

3. Spread the filling over the bottom half of each cake square and top with the remaining cake squares.

4. To make the icing, sift the icing sugar and cocoa powder together in a bowl, add the butter and mix to combine. Stir in enough milk to make an icing with a smooth coating consistency.

5. Dip the cake squares in the icing to coat completely. Roll in the coconut and dust with the drinking chocolate. Refrigerate until ready to serve.

Makes 12

Note: To make coating the cake easier, place the coconut and icing in 2 shallow dishes or cake pans. Use tongs or 2 forks to dip the cake in the icing, then place it on a wire rack set over a sheet of paper and allow it to drain for 2–3 minutes before rolling it in the coconut.

Rhubarb Strawberry Crumble

Preparation 10 mins **Cooking** 12 mins **Calories** 160 **Fat** 6g

500g rhubarb, trimmed with pink
parts only cut into 2^{1}/$_{2}$cm pieces
^{1}/$_{4}$ cup brown sugar
250g strawberries, quartered or halved

Muesli Crumble Topping
^{1}/$_{2}$ cup wholemeal flour
60g unsalted butter, cubed
^{1}/$_{2}$ cup toasted muesli
1 tbsp wheat germ
1 tbsp burghul (cracked wheat)
^{1}/$_{2}$ tsp ground nutmeg

1 Place rhubarb into a microwavable dish, sprinkle with sugar, cover and cook on high (100 percent) for 3 minutes. Stir, then cook for 2 minutes longer. Scatter strawberries over cooked rhubarb.

2 To make topping, place flour and butter in a food processor and process for 30 seconds or until mixture resembles fine breadcrumbs. Add muesli, wheat germ, burghul (cracked wheat) and nutmeg and, using the pulse, process briefly to combine.

3 Sprinkle topping over fruit and cook, on medium (50 percent) for 5 minutes.

Serves 6

Glossary

Acidulated water: water with added acid, such as lemon juice or vinegar, which prevents discolouration of ingredients, particularly fruit or vegetables. The proportion of acid to water is 1 teaspoon per 300mL.

Al dente: Italian cooking term for ingredients that are cooked until tender but still firm to the bite; usually applied to pasta.

Américaine: method of serving seafood, usually lobster and monkfish, in a sauce flavoured with olive oil, aromatic herbs, tomatoes, white wine, fish stock, brandy and tarragon.

Anglaise: cooking style for simple cooked dishes such as boiled vegetables. Assiette anglaise is a plate of cold cooked meats.

Antipasto: Italian for 'before the meal', it denotes an assortment of cold meats, vegetables and cheeses, often marinated, served as an hors d'oeuvre. A typical antipasto might include salami, prosciutto, marinated artichoke hearts, anchovy fillets, olives, tuna fish and provolone cheese.

Au gratin: food sprinkled with breadcrumbs, often covered with cheese sauce and browned until a crisp coating forms.

Bain marie: a saucepan standing in a large pan which is filled with boiling water to keep liquids at simmering point. A double boiler will do the same job.

Balsamic vinegar: a mild, extremely fragrant, wine-based vinegar made in northern Italy. Traditionally, the vinegar is aged for at least seven years in a series of casks made of various woods.

Baste: to moisten food while it is cooking by spooning or brushing on liquid or fat.

Beat: to stir thoroughly and vigorously.

Beurre manie: equal quantities of butter and flour kneaded together and added, a little at a time, to thicken a stew or casserole.

bird: see *paupiette*.

Blanc: a cooking liquid made by adding flour and lemon juice to water in order to keep certain vegetables from discolouring as they cook.

Blanch: to plunge into boiling water and then, in some cases, into cold water. Fruits and nuts are blanched to remove skin easily.

Blanquette: a white stew of lamb, veal or chicken, bound with egg yolks and cream and accompanied by onion and mushrooms.

blend: to mix thoroughly.

Bonne femme: dishes cooked in the traditional French 'housewife' style. Chicken and pork *bonne femme* are garnished with bacon, potatoes and baby onion; fish *bonne femme* with mushrooms in a white-wine sauce.

Bouquet garni: a bunch of herbs, usually consisting of sprigs of parsley, thyme, marjoram, rosemary, a bay leaf, peppercorns and cloves, tied in muslin and used to flavour stews and casseroles.

Braise: to cook whole or large pieces of poultry, game, fish, meat or vegetables in a small amount of wine, stock or other liquid in a closed pot. Often the main ingredient is first browned in fat and then cooked in a low oven or very slowly on top of the stove. Braising suits tough meats and older birds and produces a mellow, rich sauce.

Broil: the American term for grilling food.

Brown: cook in a small amount of fat until brown.

Burghul (also bulgur): a type of cracked wheat, where the kernels are steamed and dried before being crushed.

Buttered: to spread with softened or melted butter.

Butterfly: to slit a piece of food in half horizontally, cutting it almost through so that when opened it resembles butterfly wings. Chops, large prawns and thick fish fillets are often butterflied so that they cook more quickly.

Buttermilk: a tangy, low-fat cultured milk product; its slight acidity makes it an ideal marinade base for poultry.

Calzone: a semicircular pocket of pizza dough, stuffed with meat or vegetables, sealed and baked.

Caramelise: to melt sugar until it is a golden-brown syrup.

Champignons: small mushrooms, usually canned.

Chasseur: French for 'hunter'; a French cooking style in which meat and chicken dishes are cooked with mushrooms, spring onions, white wine and often tomato.

Clarify: to melt butter and drain the oil off the sediment.

Coat: to cover with a thin layer of flour, sugar, nuts, crumbs, poppy or sesame seeds, cinnamon sugar or a few of the ground spices.

Concasser: to chop coarsely, usually tomatoes.

Confit: from the French verb *confire*, meaning to preserve, food that is made into a preserve by cooking very slowly and thoroughly until tender. In the case of meat, such as duck or goose, it is cooked in its own fat, and covered with the fat so that the meat does not come into contact with the air. Vegetables such as onions are good in confit.

Consommé: a clear soup usually made from beef.

Coulis: a thin purée, usually of fresh or cooked fruit or vegetables, which is soft enough to pour (in French *couler* means 'to run'). A coulis may be rough-textured or very smooth.

Court bouillon: the liquid in which fish, poultry or meat is cooked. It usually consists of water with bay leaf, onion, carrots and salt and freshly ground black pepper to taste. Other additives may include wine, vinegar, stock, garlic or spring (green) onions.

Couscous: cereal processed from semolina into pellets, traditionally steamed and served with meat and vegetables in the classic North African stew of the same name.

Cream: to make soft, smooth and creamy by rubbing with the back of a spoon or by beating with a mixer. Usually applied to fat and sugar.

Croutons: small toasted or fried cubes of bread.

Cruciferous vegetables: certain members of the mustard, cabbage and turnip families with cross-shaped flowers and strong aromas and flavours.

Crudités: raw vegetables, cut in slices or sticks to nibble plain or with a dipping sauce, or shredded vegetables tossed as salad with a simple dressing.

Cube: to cut into small pieces with six equal sides.

Curdle: to cause milk or sauce to separate into solid and liquid. Example, overcooked egg mixtures.

Daikon radish (also called mooli): a long white Japanese radish.

Dark sesame oil (also called Oriental sesame oil): dark polyunsaturated oil with a low burning point, used for seasoning. Do not replace with lighter sesame oil.

Deglaze: to dissolve congealed cooking juices or glaze on the bottom of a pan by adding a liquid, then scraping and stirring vigorously whilst bringing the liquid to the boil. Juices may be used to make gravy or to add to sauce.

Degrease: to skim grease from the surface of liquid. If possible the liquid should be chilled so the fat solidifies. If not, skim off most of the fat with a large metal spoon, then trail strips of paper towel on the surface of the liquid to remove any remaining globules.

Devilled: a dish or sauce that is highly seasoned with a hot ingredient such as mustard, Worcestershire sauce or cayenne pepper.

Dice: to cut into small cubes.

Dietary fibre: a plant-cell material that is undigested or only partially digested in the human body, but which promotes healthy digestion of other food matter.

Dissolve: mix a dry ingredient with liquid until absorbed.

Dredge: to coat with a dry ingredient, such as flour or sugar.

Drizzle: to pour in a fine thread-like stream over a surface.

Dust: to sprinkle or coat lightly with flour or icing sugar.

Dutch oven: a heavy casserole with a lid usually made from cast iron or pottery.

Emulsion: a mixture of two liquids that are not mutually soluble; for example, oil and water.

Entrée: in Europe, the 'entry' or hors d'oeuvre; in North America entree means the main course.

Fenugreek: a small, slender annual herb of the pea family. The seeds are spice. Ground fenugreek has a strong maple sweetness, spicy but bitter flavour and an aroma of burnt sugar.

Fillet: special cut of beef, lamb, pork or veal; breast of poultry and game; fish cut off the bone lengthwise.

Flake: to break into small pieces with a fork.

Flame: to ignite warmed alcohol over food.

Fold in: a gentle, careful combining of a light or delicate mixture with a heavier mixture, using a metal spoon.

Frenched: when fat and gristle is scraped and cut from meat on a bone, leaving the meaty part virtually fat free.

Fricassé: a dish in which poultry, fish or vegetables are bound together with a white or velouté sauce. In Britain and the United States, the name applies to an old-fashioned dish of chicken in a creamy sauce.

Galangal: A member of the ginger family, commonly known as Laos or Siamese ginger. It has a peppery taste with overtones of ginger.

Galette: sweet or savoury mixture shaped as a flat round.

Ganache: a filling or glaze made of full cream, chocolate, and/or other flavourings, often used to sandwich the layers of gourmet chocolate cakes

Garnish: to decorate food, usually with something edible.

Gastrique: caramelised sugar deglazed with vinegar and used in fruit-flavoured savoury sauces, in such dishes as duck with orange.

Ghee: butter, clarified by boiling. Commonly used in Indian cooking.

Glaze: a thin coating of beaten egg, syrup or aspic which is brushed over pastry, fruits or cooked meats.

Gluten: a protein in flour that is developed when dough is kneaded, making the dough elastic.

Gratin: a dish cooked in the oven or under the grill so that it develops a brown crust. Breadcrumbs or cheese may be sprinkled on top first. Shallow gratin dishes ensure a maximum area of crust.

Grease: to rub or brush lightly with oil or fat.

Infuse: to immerse herbs, spices or other flavourings in hot liquid to flavour it. Infusion takes 2–5 minutes depending on the flavouring. The liquid should be very hot but not boiling.

Jardinière: a garnish of garden vegetables, typically carrots, pickling onions, French beans and turnips.

Joint: to cut poultry, game or small animals into serving pieces by dividing at the joint.

Julienne: to cut food into match-like strips.

Lights: lungs of an animal, used in various meat preparations such as pates and faggots.

Line: to cover the inside of a container with paper, to protect or aid in removing mixture.

Knead: to work dough using heel of hand with a pressing motion, while stretching and folding the dough.

Macerate: to soak food in liquid to soften.

Marinade: a seasoned liquid, usually an oil and acid mixture, in which meats or other foods are soaked to soften and give more flavour.

Marinara: Italian 'sailor's style' cooking that does not apply to any particular combination of ingredients. Marinara tomato sauce for pasta is the most familiar.

Marinate: to let food stand in a marinade to season and tenderise.

Mask: to cover cooked food with sauce.

Melt: to heat until liquified.

Mince: to grind into very small pieces.

Mix: to combine ingredients by stirring.

Monounsaturated fats: one of three types of fats found in foods. It is believed these fats do not raise the level of cholesterol in the blood.

Naan: a slightly leavened bread used in Indian cooking.

Niçoise: a garnish of tomatoes, garlic and black olives; a salad with anchovy, tuna and French beans is typical.

Noisette: small 'nut' of lamb cut from boned loin or rack that is rolled, tied and cut in neat slices. Noisette also means flavoured with hazelnuts, or butter cooked to a nut brown colour.

Non-reactive pan: a cooking pan whose surface does not chemically react with food. Materials used include stainless steel, enamel, glass and some alloys.

Normande: a cooking style for fish, with a garnish of prawn, mussels and mushrooms in a white-wine cream sauce; for poultry and meat, a sauce with cream, calvados and apple.

Olive oil: various grades of oil extracted from olives. Extra virgin olive oil has a full, fruity flavour and the lowest acidity. Virgin olive oil is slightly higher in acidity and lighter in flavour. Pure olive oil is a processed blend of olive oils and has the highest acidity and lightest taste.

Panade: a mixture for binding stuffings and dumplings, notably quenelles (fish rissoles), often of choux pastry or simply breadcrumbs. A panade may also be made of frangipane, puréed potatoes or rice.

Papillote: to cook food in oiled or buttered greasepoof paper or aluminum foil. Also a decorative frill to cover bone ends of chops and poultry drumsticks.

Parboil: to boil or simmer until part cooked (i.e. cooked further than when blanching).

Pare: to cut away outside covering.

Pâté: a paste of meat or seafood used as a spread for toast or crackers.

Paupiette: a thin slice of meat, poultry or fish spread with a savoury stuffing and rolled. In the United States this is also called 'bird' and in Britain an 'olive'.

Peel: to strip away outside covering.

Plump: to soak in liquid or moisten thoroughly until full and round.

Poach: to simmer gently in enough hot liquid to cover, using care to retain shape of food.

Polyunsaturated fat: one of the three types of fats found in food. These exist in large quantities in such vegetable oils as safflower, sunflower, corn and soya bean. These fats lower the level of cholesterol in the blood.

Purée: a smooth paste, usually of vegetables or fruits, made by putting foods through a sieve, food mill or liquefying in a blender or food processor.

Ragout: traditionally a well-seasoned, rich stew containing meat, vegetables and wine. Nowadays, a term applied to any stewed mixture.

Ramekins: small oval or round individual baking dishes.

Reconstitute: to put moisture back into dehydrated foods by soaking in liquid.

Reduce: to cook over a very high heat, uncovered, until the liquid is reduced by evaporation.

Refresh: to cool hot food quickly, either under running water or by plunging it into iced water, to stop it cooking. Particularly for vegetables and occasionally for shellfish.

Rice vinegar: mild, fragrant vinegar that is less sweet than cider vinegar and not as harsh as distilled malt vinegar. Japanese rice vinegar is milder than the Chinese variety.

Roulade: a piece of meat, usually pork or veal, that is spread with stuffing, rolled and often braised or poached. A roulade may also be a sweet or savoury mixture that is baked in a Swiss-roll tin or paper case, filled with a contrasting filling, and rolled.

Roux: A binding for sauces, made with flour and butter or another fatty substance, to which a hot liquid is added. A roux-based sauce may be white, blond or brown, depending on how the butter has been cooked.

Rubbing-in: a method of incorporating fat into flour, by use of fingertips only. Also incorporates air into mixture.

Safflower oil: the vegetable oil that contains the highest proportion of polyunsaturated fats.

Salsa: a juice derived from the main ingredient being cooked, or a sauce added to a dish to enhance its flavour. In Italy the term is often used for pasta sauces; in Mexico the name usually applies to uncooked sauces served as an accompaniment, especially to corn chips.

Saturated fats: one of the three types of fats found in foods. These exist in large quantities in animal products, coconut and palm oils; they raise the level of cholesterol in the blood. As high cholesterol levels may cause heart disease, saturated-fat consumption is recommended to be less than 15 percent of calories provided by the daily diet.

Sauté: to cook or brown in small amount of hot fat.

Scald: to bring just to boiling point, usually for milk. Also to rinse with boiling water.

School prawns: delicious eaten just on their own. Smaller prawn than bay, tiger or king. They have a mild flavour, low oiliness and high moisture content, they make excellent cocktails.

Score: to mark food with cuts, notches or lines to prevent curling or to make food more attractive.

Sear: to brown surface quickly over high heat in hot dish.

Seasoned flour: flour with salt and pepper added.

Sift: to shake a dry, powdered substance through a sieve or sifter to remove any lumps and give lightness.

Simmer: to cook food gently in liquid that bubbles steadily just below boiling point so that the food cooks in even heat without breaking up.

Singe: to quickly flame poultry to remove all traces of feathers after plucking.

Skim: to remove a surface layer (often of impurities and scum) from a liquid with a metal spoon or small ladle.

Slivered: sliced in long, thin pieces, usually refers to nuts, especially almonds.

Souse: to cover food, particularly fish, in wine vinegar and spices and cook slowly; the food is cooled in the same liquid. Sousing gives food a pickled flavour.

Steep: to soak in warm or cold liquid in order to soften food and draw out strong flavours or impurities.

Stir-fry: to cook thin slices of meat and vegetable over a high heat in a small amount of oil, stirring constantly to even cooking in a short time. Traditionally cooked in a wok; however, a heavy-based frying pan may be used.

Stock: the liquid that results from cooking meat, bones and/or vegetables in water to make a base for soups and other recipes. You can substitute stock cubes for fresh bouillon, but those on a reduced sodium diet will need to take note of the salt content on the packet.

Stud: to adorn with; for example, baked ham studded with whole cloves.

Sugo: an Italian sauce made from the liquid or juice extracted from fruit or meat during cooking.

Sweat: to cook sliced or chopped food, usually vegetables, in a little fat and no liquid over very low heat. Foil is pressed on top so that the food steams in its own juices, usually before being added to other dishes.

Thicken: to make a liquid thicker by mixing together arrowroot, cornflour or flour with an equal amount of cold water and pouring it into hot liquid, cooking and stirring until thickened.

Timbale: a creamy mixture of vegetables or meat baked in a mould. French for 'kettledrum'; also denotes a drum-shaped baking dish.

Toss: to gently mix ingredients with two forks or fork and spoon.

Total fat: the individual daily intake of all three fats previously described in this glossary. Nutritionists recommend that fats provide no more than 35 percent of the energy in the diet.

Vine leaves: tender, lightly flavoured leaves of the grapevine, used in ethnic cuisine as wrappers for savoury mixtures. As the leaves are usually packed in brine, they should be well rinsed before use.

Whip: to beat rapidly, incorporate air and produce expansion.

Zest: thin outer layer of citrus fruits containing the aromatic citrus oil. It is usually thinly pared with a vegetable peeler, or grated with a zester or grater to separate it from the bitter white pith underneath.

Weights and Measures

Cooking is not an exact science. You do not require finely calibrated scales, pipettes and scientific equipment to cook, yet the variety of measures in countries have confused many a good cook.

Although different in the recipes weights are given for ingredients such as meats, fish, poultry and some vegetables, in normal cooking a few ounces or grams one way or another will not affect the success of your dish.

Although recipes have been tested using the Australian Standard 250mL cup, 20mL tablespoon (tbsp) and 5mL teaspoon (tsp), they will work just as well with the US and Canadian 8fl oz cup, or the UK 300mL cup. We have used graduated cup measures in preference to tablespoon measures so that proportions are always the same. Where tablespoon measures have been given, they are not crucial measures, so using the smaller tablespoon of the US or UK will not affect the recipe's success. At least all three countries agree on the teaspoon size.

For breads, cakes and pastries, the only area which might cause concern is where eggs are used, as proportions will then vary. If working with a 250mL or 300mL cup, use large eggs (65g/2^1/4oz), adding a little more liquid to the recipe for 300mL cup measures if it seems necessary. Use medium-sized eggs (55g/2oz) with an 8fl oz cup measure. A graduated set of measuring cups and spoons is recommended for measuring dry ingredients. Remember to level the ingredients in the measure to ensure an accurate quantity.

English Measures

English measurements are all similar to Australian with two exceptions: the English cup measures 300mL/10^1/2 fl oz, whereas the American and Australian cup measures 250mL/8^3/4fl oz. The English tablespoon (the Australian dessertspoon) measures 14.8mL/^{1}/2 fl oz against Australian tablespoon of 20mL/^{3}/4fl oz. The Imperial measurement is 20fl oz to the pint, 40fl oz a quart and 160fl oz one gallon.

American Measures

The American reputed pint is 16fl oz, a quart is equal to 32fl oz and the American gallon equals 128fl oz. The American tablespoon is equal to 14.8mL/^{1}/2 fl oz, while the teaspoon is 5mL/^{1}/6 fl oz. The cup measure is 250 mL/8^3/4 fl oz.

Dry Measures

All the measures are level, so when you have filled a cup or spoon, level it off with the edge of a knife. The scale below is the 'cook's equivalent'; it is not an exact conversion of metric to imperial measurement. To calculate the exact metric equivalent yourself, multiply ounces by 28.349523 to obtain grams, or divide grams by 28.349523 to obtain ounces.

Metric grams (g), kilograms (kg)	Imperial ounces (oz), pound (lb)
15g	^{1}/2oz
20g	^{1}/3oz
30g	1oz
55g	2oz
85g	3oz
115g	4oz/^{1}/4lb
125g	4^1/2oz
140/145g	5oz
170g	6oz
200g	7oz
225g	8oz/^{1}/2lb
315g	11oz
340g	12oz/^{3}/4lb
370g	13oz
400g	14oz
425g	15oz
455g	16oz/1lb
1,000g/1 kg	35.3oz/2.2lb
1.5kg	3.33lb

Oven Temperatures

The Celsius temperatures given here are not exact; they have been rounded off and are given as a guide only. Follow the manufacturer's oven guide, relating it to the temperature description given in the recipe. Remember gas ovens are hottest at the top, electric ovens at the bottom and convection-fan forced ovens are usually even throughout. We have included Regulo numbers for gas cookers which may assist. To convert °C to °F multiply °C by 9 and divide by 5 then add 32.

	C°	F°	Gas mark
Very slow	120	250	1
Slow	150	300	2
Moderately slow	160	325	3
Moderate	180	350	4
Moderately hot	190–200	370–400	5–6
Hot	210–220	410–440	6–7
Very hot	230	450	8
Super hot	250–290	475–500	9–10

Cup Measurements

One Australian cup (250mL) is equal to the following weights.

	Metric	Imperial
Almonds, flaked	85g	3oz
Almonds, kernel	155g	5$\frac{1}{2}$oz
Almonds, slivered, ground	125g	4$\frac{1}{2}$oz
Apples, dried, chopped	125g	4$\frac{1}{2}$oz
Apricots, dried, chopped	190g	6$\frac{3}{4}$oz
Breadcrumbs, packet	125g	4$\frac{1}{2}$oz
Breadcrumbs, soft	55g	2oz
Cheese, grated	115g	4oz
Chocbits	155$\frac{1}{2}$g	5oz
Coconut, desiccated	90g	3oz
Cornflakes	30g	1oz
Currants	155$\frac{1}{2}$g	5oz
Flour	115g	4oz
Fruit, dried (mixed, sultanas etc)	170g	6 oz
Ginger, crystallised, glace	250g	8oz
Honey, treacle, golden syrup	315g	11oz
Mixed peel	225g	8oz
Nuts, chopped	115g	4oz
Prunes, chopped	225g	8oz
Rice, cooked	155g	5$\frac{1}{2}$oz
Rice, uncooked	225g	8oz
Rolled oats	90g	3oz
Sesame seeds	115g	4oz
Shortening (butter, margarine)	225g	8oz
Sugar, brown	155g	5$\frac{1}{2}$oz
Sugar, granulated or caster	225g	8oz
Sugar, sifted icing	155g	5$\frac{1}{2}$oz
Wheatgerm	60g	2oz

Length

Some of us have trouble converting imperial length to metric. In this scale, measures have been rounded off to the easiest figures. To convert inches to centimetres exactly, multiply inches by 2.54. One inch equals 25.4 millimetres and 1 millimetre equals 0.03937 inches.

Cake Dish Sizes

Metric	15cm	18cm	20cm	23cm
Imperial	6in	7in	8in	9in

Loaf Dish Sizes

Metric	23 x 12cm	25 x 8cm	28 x 18cm
Imperial	9 x 5in	10 x 3in	11 x 7in

Liquid Measures

Metric millilitres (mL)	Imperial fluid ounce (fl oz)	Cup and Spoon
5mL	$\frac{1}{6}$fl oz	1 teaspoon
20mL	$\frac{2}{3}$fl oz	1 tablespoon
30mL	1fl oz	1 tbsp + 2 tsp
55mL	2fl oz	
63mL	2$\frac{1}{4}$fl oz	$\frac{1}{4}$ cup
85mL	3fl oz	
115mL	4fl oz	
125mL	4$\frac{1}{2}$fl oz	$\frac{1}{2}$ cup
150mL	5$\frac{1}{4}$fl oz	
188mL	6$\frac{2}{3}$fl oz	$\frac{3}{4}$ cup
225mL	8fl oz	
250mL	8$\frac{3}{4}$fl oz	1 cup
300mL	10$\frac{1}{2}$fl oz	
370mL	13fl oz	
400mL	14fl oz	
438mL	15$\frac{1}{2}$fl oz	1$\frac{3}{4}$ cups
455mL	16fl oz	
500mL	17$\frac{1}{2}$fl oz	2 cups
570mL	20fl oz	
1 litre	35.3fl oz	4 cups

Length Measures

Metric millimetres (mm), centimetres (cm)	Imperial inches (in), feet (ft)
5mm, 0.5cm	$\frac{1}{4}$in
10mm, 1.0cm	$\frac{1}{2}$in
20mm, 2.0cm	$\frac{3}{4}$in
2.5cm	1in
5cm	2in
7$\frac{1}{2}$cm	3in
10cm	4in
12$\frac{1}{2}$cm	5in
15cm	6in
18cm	7in
20cm	8in
23cm	9in
25cm	10in
28cm	11in
30cm	12in, 1 foot

Index